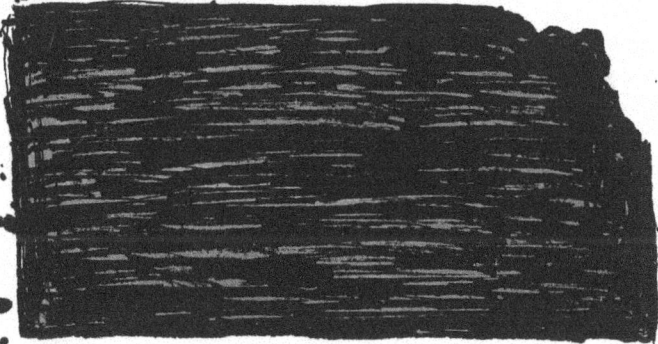

CERTAIN STREETS
at an
UNCERTAIN HOUR

poems by

Jeff Tigchelaar

illustrations by

Charlotte Pemberton

Edited by Dennis Etzel, Jr.

Printed by Lightning Source
Book design: Jeremy Shellhorn
Illustrations: Charlotte Pemberton

Woodley Press
Department of English
Washburn University
Topeka, KS 66621
washburn.edu/reference/woodley-press/index.html

ISBN: 978-0-9908128-0-7

for
Jana, Charlotte & Sam

Contents

1. Abandon

Report to William Stafford   13
You Are Here   14
from Day Notes: Lawrence, Kansas   15
All That's Happened since Kristen Spilled Beer on Our Carpet   19
Least Weasel (*Mustela nivalis*)   20
Poem on Placard for Placard for Statue   22
Reading at the Raven   24
Today We Saw a Man   26
Abandon   27
Stop   28
Kansas Interlude   31

2. A Cross between Mythical and Real

The Planes   35
Fly Frontier   36
The Thing about Dying   37
Animals Were Looking at Me   38
It   39
Dude, You Killed a Marsupial   41
George Brett's Labradoodle   44
On Its Side   46
There's This Thing   47
It's Totally a Thing (or, The Jackalope Question)   49

3. A Sign, Perhaps, that All Is Well

(In Which I Have Substituted) 'Poets' for 'Stones'   53
Mourn the Cicadas   54
I Am Trying to Help You   57
The Transfer   58
The House Teetered On / The Edge of Absurdity   59
Postcard from Rose, 3, to Charlotte, 4, in Lawrence   60
Letter to Howard Payne   61
My Kin, My Country, My Casserole (Double Abecedarian)   63
Without (Double Abecedarian)   64
Zig Is My Name – Call This My Cantata (Double Abecedarian) 65

4. You Are Here

It Never Happens   69
Ours Was the Best-Dressed Scarecrow   70
My Topeka Writers Group Leader Passed Out   71
William C. Quantrill   73
Torn/ado   74
Bacon Raised   75
For the Love of God, Sean Kuno   77
February: Mass Street   78
"Dust in the Wind" on Repeat (January 2011)   79
Song for 2013   80
Postcard, with Arrows   81

Acknowledgements   84
About the author   87
About the illustrator   87

Just the ordinary days, please.
I wouldn't want them any better.

William Stafford, "Notes for the Program"

In my book I fold these things I saw
and a few other things that shadows brought around...

William Stafford, "Writing It Down"

1. Abandon

Report to William Stafford

Kansas, 2011

The poets were all
but defeated

They still wrote
still followed
the golden thread
as you said
but only for themselves
it seemed

Which is all just
an artsy way of saying
We are now the only state in America without
an Arts Council and man it's embarrassing

*

If you were still around maybe you'd go
find the governor and read him
something full of kindness and light
that might change his mind and his life

*

Your art has had and will have better days

I bought your book at a Borders
I'm sorry to say
it had been there awhile
I could tell

though you I'm sure would not have
minded the dust

I found it on a back shelf

Other books had gathered around
as if to listen

You Are Here

Light drips down
from the capitol dome. Coffee
flows up through
veins, and all is not for
nothing, governor, nothing
is for naught when it's made
for the benefit of everyone and the self
walking certain streets at
an uncertain hour

from Day Notes: Lawrence, Kansas (2012-2013)

At the new Starbucks on Sixth and Wakarusa
a woman is talking on her phone,
taking frantic notes and flipping through
a folder. *No, no,* she says,
he's supposed to be protecting us

On the way here I saw a turtle
flattened in the road. It was
on its back and the size of a pillow

The money will come from ATMs
all over the world, the woman says

It seems like someone could've swerved

*

Found a crumpled check on the ground
made out to Jennifer Jimboy for $7.23
from the Huna Totem Corporation,
Juneau, Alaska, dated February 15, 2011

Locked my bike to a light-pole; walked into Wescoe Hall

Got hopelessly lost in Wescoe Hall

Saw the poet Kenneth Irby, who works
in Wescoe Hall, get lost in Wescoe Hall

Got coffee in the basement food-court and resolved to keep trying

Finally found the Department of English. Dropped off
some poems for the *Coal City Review*

Dropped my coffee on the Department of English
carpeting; picked up the cup and kept walking. (I don't think
anyone saw.) It made a stain
that looked to me like Florida without its keys

Wondered why Jennifer Jimboy didn't want that check
– or whether she maybe just dropped it

Pictured her crumpling up the check
and screaming You can take this
seven twenty-three and shove it

*

Ran out into a field and punched a hay bale

Was out for a jog and saw it sitting there and thought
If I go punch that hay bale, at least
I'll be able to say I punched a hay bale

Opened the garage door to quick bring out the garbage
and the little neighbor boy was in our driveway on his scooter
and I'll be honest, the first thing I thought was
Great: there's *that* little fucker

Then of course he started talking:
Hi Jeff what are you doing Jeff I like your new hair Jeff
by which he meant my new lack of hair

and I suppose the real question for me
is Why have you become Old Cranky
when you live in a place
where someone knows you by name
and is happy to see you
and can tell something about you has changed?

All That's Happened since Kristen Spilled Beer on Our Carpet

Grandpa died. We quick made plans to pack and fly to Michigan. The luggage got lost in Milwaukee. Everyone and everything arrived, eventually. The day after getting back to Kansas, we turned around and drove to Chicago for that conference. Virginia was a no-show, and we were sad about that; we're pretty sure we know what it meant. We picked up the kids in Iowa, where they'd been stashed with your parents. Sam had blown out his pants, and your dad changed a diaper for the first time in his life. "If anyone is changed, it's me," he said. Halfway through Missouri the family meltdown began. It's one thing that's never unexpected. We solved it with a ten-dollar pizza from a Casey's. We sat in the car and ate it in the dark. We didn't know gas station food could be that good. The silence was nice at first, but when it was too much I slipped in my favorite CD. You said "Now is not the time for Sinead O'Connor." I disagreed, and grabbed the last two pieces of pizza. I sulked for the next few hours. The children made us listen to Yo Gabba Gabba. Somehow we got home, and the Tigers got Prince Fielder. Whitney Houston died in her bathtub, and was only 48 years old. I had no idea she was that young. I'm in my thirties, and she was Whitney Houston already when I was about five. I'll never forget the time she guest-starred on Silver Spoons. "I think I'm in love with Whitney Houston," said Dexter, and then of course I was, too. Good Lord. Now Kristen's gone, and the stain is still here. What has it been, a month?

Least Weasel *(Mustela nivalis)*

Natural History Museum, University of Kansas

I'm right there with you, little guy.
Sometimes I feel like
you: "the smallest
carnivore in the world."

Poor fella, I say aloud
to the critter encased in glass. (It's Monday,
no one's around, so really it's okay that I'm conversing
with a tiny stuffed mammal.)

I tell him there's something
somewhere in the Bible
on the least being first,
        or maybe it's the last being first
        and the least being blessed.
Either way, it's good news for us.

    But then, further down
on my little friend's placard,
I read *this* bit of information:
        "The least weasel is known to take on
        much larger creatures,
          the cotton rat, for example,
*by wrapping its legs around the prey
and delivering a swift bite at the base of the skull.*"

Least weasels, it seems, don't need pep talks
from the likes of me.

I turn to leave;
        but as I walk   I find I've got
this sudden, new
resolve:
  I exit the building
        and look for something big.

Poem on Placard for Placard for Statue

The Spencer Museum of Art

Never mind the Winslow Homer, the Albrecht Dürer, the Georgia O'Keeffe.
Forget the Chihuly, the Rossetti, the Grant Wood.
What captured my attention – though it failed
at first to even catch my eye – was the placard
to the left of the placard
to the left of the statue
of Saint Damian.

Circle of Ignaz Günther
Germany, 1725-1775
Saint Damian, circa 1770-1775
painted and gilt lindenwood
museum purchase, 1950.0091
       reads the placard for the saint.

Label for Saint Damian, 2008
toner on cardstock
museum purchase, 2008.1072
       reads the placard for the placard for the saint.

'Remake Your Museum' project, Spring 2008…challenged students to create
labels for objects in the museum not traditionally considered
to be art objects
       reads the placard explaining the placard
       for the placard
       for the saint.

'Label for Saint Damian' reflects the mores of late 20th to early 21st century museum label-
ing. Starkly minimalist in its physical construction, the label diverges from a purely utilitarian
form
only through the addition of a discreet beveled edge
       reads the sign containing Daniel Hogan's
       artist statement for his winning entry, the placard
       for the placard for Saint Damian.
              Hogan then goes on to say that

such simplicity, the antithesis of a rococo picture frame, reinforces the label's
subservience to the artwork it describes

before continuing at even greater length
his explication of the newfound piece,
causing one to think
more about a label
than one has presumably ever thought before – more
about the placard and its placard, perhaps, than about
the statue
of poor Saint Damian.

Good old
Damian – the original
work of art; the one
the placards
were meant to serve:
Damian, who guards the gallery's gateway,
a post he's manned for half a century;
who looms with towering dignity
as soon as one enters the room;
who stands in his ancient robe,
cracked and gray yet trimmed in gold;
whose hand curls to a claw,
as if to clutch some missing thing
or grasp a distant thought;
whose other hand holds a gilded chalice;
whose bearded face bears a visage
somewhere between anguish and bliss –

he of the upturned eyes, he
of the unchanged gaze:
what must he think of this shift
in focus?

Reading at the Raven (a quintuple ekphrastic)

five posters: The Raven Book Store, Lawrence

Mystery! Mystery! My mind, it's
        wandering when I should be listening
to the reading: to this poor poet
standing there, trying
to share some hard-wrought lines
                      but instead
I'm watching the detectives – watching the detectives watch
over us from the sky (or, the wall): five detectives
up above, spying on us all
down here. Five detectives,
left to right – catching us
unawares.

-

"A detective of distinction," Poirot
peeks with one eye, one
surprised and angry eye. The other is hidden
by his bowler hat. And his moustache mimics
his black bowtie. And his left hand grips a cane.
              And his brain
      holds all
our secrets.

-

Sherlock Holmes – "still
so clever" – Sherlock Holmes
accuses with his finger, his
            confidently extended pointer. Watson
peers over Sherlock's shoulder. Watson
appears concerned. Could it be true
      that Holmes has gotten one wrong?
He's blaming me.
He's blaming you.

-

Simenon's Maigret: he taunts us with his eyes.
He's far from being in a hurried state, and further
still from one of concern.
He's found a match.

He knows what we're about.
    His flame burns and burns
but never goes out.

-

Inspector Alleyn – Inspector
Roderick Alleyn: we don't have to guess
what's on his mind. Despite
a known weakness for the drink,
there's something else
that makes him even weaker.
      His wayward eye tonight has fallen
on the mysterious shape of a lady.
It's forms like these
of which he's the chief inspector.

-

Campion stands in a ray of light,
with a man in black at his back.
Campion. Campion. Who the hell
is Campion? And is he as much of a champ
as his name would have us believe?

I want to believe in Campion.
I want to Google Campion. So I do
and now it is I
who am doing the finding: Campion, it seems,
also goes by other names:
Mornington Dove. Mornington Dodd. Christopher Twelvetrees.
The Honourable Tootles Ash.
Campion has a manservant
by the name of Magersfontein Lugg – "an uncouth,
rough-and-tumble fellow," it's said. A former burglar, balding.

Campion is thin, wears glasses; he's "affable, inoffensive and bland,
with a deceptively blank and unintelligent expression."

Campion: Campion
              …c'est moi! I am Campion
and Campion is me. I am
      a detective, and I'm watching
you, watching me.

Today We Saw a Man

take a coffee cup from a trash can
and drink what had been left

and this was right in front of
the Starbucks, right
in Lawrence, Kansas, where
somehow there's a man who doesn't have
enough to eat

and this was right in front of
my kids, who somehow had
no questions

Abandon

Someone, this morning,
at the vacant gas station –
the long-deserted Phillips 66
with tall weeds
and for-sale signs
and broken concrete
and no prices on the marquee –
trying to fill up

*

Dropping Sam off
at pre-school I saw
a mom in a minivan
dabbing her eyes

*

Leaving the lot
I see a pink Cadillac SUV
and laugh and laugh

Stop

I'm at a truck stop in central Kansas staring at a t-shirt display while my three-year-old marvels at a claw game I'm totally not letting him play. Tequila makes my clothes fall off, says one shirt. Rebel born, rebel bred, I'll be a rebel until I'm dead, says another, with a skeleton face and Confederate flag. A black man walks past us toward the Huddle House diner. Shower customer seven, your shower's now ready, the ceiling speakers say.

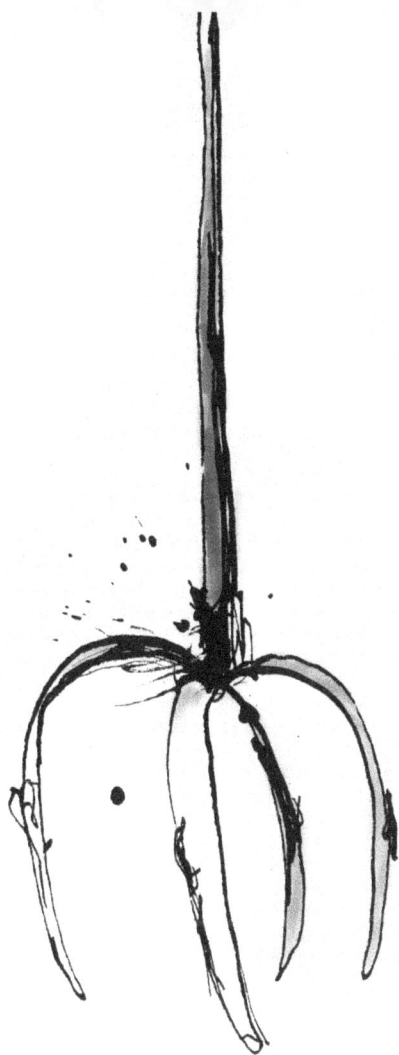

Kansas Interlude

Kansas was heaven
and Kansas was hell

and Kansas was the time
I couldn't tell

2. A Cross between Mythical and Real

The Planes

Arrowhead Stadium, Kansas City, November

My first pro football game.
I came for the tailgating scene.
I'd fallen asleep five times by the fourth.
I'm unused to beer before noon.

I snapped awake
when fans began
to finally get excited:
a paper plane
making its way
slowly from great heights
down toward the field of play.

Fly Frontier

I'm in a manmade capsule hurtling through the sky
so if I die I probably deserve it.
It's early
and still dark, but Kansas City
is all lit up. There's a yawping
wolf outside my window
painted on the wingtip,
eyes closed, muzzle up, how whimsical.
No, how foreboding. And why is it so
choppy? God, we've only
just taken off. Now we're drastically tilting
and the plane wing looks like a slide.
If this were a dream, I'd step out
and plunge into the darkness of a Monday
and fall until everything was light

The Thing about Dying

Today on a remote trail I encountered
a man, and as we were passing he said
Beautiful morning
and I said Yes it is
and he said I bet
you didn't think you'd die today
and I said No I didn't but
it *would* happen this way, wouldn't it

but he didn't really say
the thing about dying; that part
was only in my head.
What he actually said was
It's my first time out here! I'm Keith!
To which I replied
Ah! Nice! I'm Jeff! Second time. Great spot. Enjoy the trail!
Keith was very smiley and heavyset,
with a white beard and a golden retriever
who was just as smiley as Keith
and who should've been on a leash, but oh well

Animals Were Looking at Me

One neat thing about where I live in Kansas
is that you can turn north off Sixth
just past the Walmart and the strip malls,
go about half a mile, round a bend, take a left,
turn into the dirt lot with the Martin Park sign,
get out and walk a quarter-mile on the path, and all of a sudden
you come out on this rural road
and you're totally in the country, which
you can tell because animals
are looking right at you: geese, a goat,
a white horse with some sort of jacket,
a little donkey,
an alpaca.

It's the strangest
kind of eye contact

and it's impossibly quiet

but then a leashless pit bull comes charging
and only stops when called
by its owner from the window of a trailer
and soon you'll begin – I'll begin – breathing again

and the dog, dejected, will amble home
and I'll unfreeze and keep walking,
the horse having now turned its back,
the alpaca now rolling on the ground,
no longer interested in me.

It

That is what you have to do, before you kill…
You have to create an *it*.
                    – Margaret Atwood

I don't think he planned to kill me. I mean, the man
resembled Flanders, of Simpsons fame: Neighborly Ned,
mustache and all, *Hidely-ho*. He had a small dog
called Lucy. And that's what he did –
called Lucy – when Lucy came
after me. And that's when
he called me
an it.
        I, out
for a late-night walk; Lucy, out
for a late-night squat, under
Ned's watchful eye – Lucy
charges the passerby,
yours truly, this
interrupter of canine duty;
Ned cries "Leave it,
Lucy! Lucy,
leave it
alone."

It did
kind of kill me. In a sense.
    Having been reduced
            to no more than a pronoun
for an object, animal, or baby,
    I wandered the streets
of Kansas, shirking
    all further contact
with man or beast.
        The rest of the evening
    was a blur.
I no longer knew
        who I was.
I looked at my hands
    now curled into claws.
I drew back my head
    and pawed at the moon

and cried "Ned!
You've made me
                a monster.
        You've made me
a piece
        of meat!"

                Somehow I found
        my way home. My wife, still up,
said I looked a bit frazzled.

        Unable to speak,
    I shrugged. Grunted.
And curled on the couch to sleep.

Dude, You Killed a Marsupial

for my brother

What I've learned about opossums
since that gruesome ordeal
a few summers back
is that:

* they have hand-shaped paws

* they have prehensile tails

* they are on display (one of them, at least)
at the Prairie Park Nature Center

which means someone saw fit
to keep one alive
for educational purposes.

Someone whose job
is animals.

The Nature People seemed to think opossums
have something to offer!

* The one I saw had its own litter box. It knew
how to use a litter box, just like
a cat.

* In spite of resembling a rodent, the opossum
is North America's only marsupial.

* They pouch their young!

* You killed America's kangaroo!

And I helped. In the capture, at least. Though
in our defense, it was wreaking havoc
in mom and dad's garage.

* Opossums can give birth to up to thirteen babies
after a gestation of only seven days.
They have two litters per year.

* You may have saved mom and dad
from later having 26 opossums in their garage.

* At three months old, the babies
emerge from the pouch
and ride on the mother's back.

Precious!
Right?

* If startled, opossums have a faint reflex
known as "playing dead."

Maybe it was
only playing

George Brett's Labradoodle

May 30, 2012

George Brett's dog is missing,
and I intend to find him.

Or her. I'm not sure at this point
whether it's a boy or a girl. All I know
is that it's George Brett's dog,
and man, it's gone.

           George Brett tweeted
just seconds ago, says my wife,
that his beloved black Labradoodle had up
and taken off, and he – George Brett

– the greatest Kansas City Royal
of all time! – George Brett – the Hall
-of-Famer! – George Brett – one
of the finest third-baseman
ever to play the game! –

George Brett wanted to enlist the public's help
in finding his much-loved Charlie.

      Charlie! So it's a he. Probably.
And there would be
"a reward"
for whoever so happens
to find Charlie.
      And Charlie lives
in Kansas City. Mission Hills
near Tomahawk and Seneca.
      And we, we live
a half hour west. George Brett
and George Brett's dog, presumably,
are within 30 miles of where we now sit.
          Of where we now stand.
      Of where we now rise
to the occasion,
to the call, where we go
help a man in need, a man

who is missing a friend
who is missing – a man
who happens
to be George Brett
but who's not beyond asking
for help, not beyond seeking
the assistance of people
like you and me.

So – off we go: off to be
      hero to a hero.

          Here, Charlie!

On Its Side

in the ditch that had given me new shoes
– a barely worn pair of New Balances, that is,
complete with costly sole inserts – shoes
precisely my size, discarded
inexplicably and which
I'd since washed repeatedly
but now was wearing,
which might have been
what led me to walk
back out to the spot,
to return to the scene of discovery and see
if the universe had anything else
to deliver –

on its side in that same ditch
was an animal the size
and shape of a dog,
a large black dog that would have remained
forever a dog if I hadn't seen
the cloven hoof
and the teeth
the size
of a lipstick tube
shooting up from the mouth like new growth

There's This Thing

and I don't know what it is
but I haul it all around
because it's attached to my hand.

There's this cloth that's wrapped tight
'round my arm: bright orange cloth all the way
past my elbow and affixed
to some mesh wiring.
A lot of mesh wiring.
I have to drag it behind me. It's like I've got
a giant-mesh-wire-cage arm! Sometimes I turn around
and I'm like *Oh God what the – ?* All these years
and still it catches me off guard.
It gives me some leeway in crowds, at least.

The cage is teardrop-shaped
and large enough to house
(and does in fact house)
a five-foot, oh, how should I say it.
Starfish-squid. (As if there were some
better way!) Sometimes when I feel whimsical
I twirl it, my starfish-squid – just spin and spin
and give it the sensation of flight.
But I know
what that thing really needs is water.

after Damia Smith, "Catharsis," (steel, cotton, beeswax;
Kansas University, Metalsmithing/Jewelry, 2013)

It's Totally a Thing (or, The Jackalope Question)

Child 1: What do you mean, it's not real?

Child 2: Yeah, why would it be on the wall at the Nature Center if it's not real?

Parent 1: It's a thing –

Parent 2: See?

Parent 1: Let me finish. It's a big Victorian thing –

Parent 2: Jackalopes are *British*?

Parent 1: Let me finish. It was a thing in the Victorian era – sometimes as a party gag, but other times to pretend they discovered something new. But it's not *really* real, kids.

Child 2: How do you know?

Parent 2: Yeah, how could you say it's not real, if we're talking about it? How could I be picturing it right now, in my head, if it's not real?

Parent 1: Okay, let's put it this way: It's mythical.

Child 1: I think it might be real.

Child 2: They have it on the wall at the Prairie Park Nature Center!

Child 1: I saw it too. So it's real. It's just a cross between a jackrabbit and an antelope.

Parent 1: Thus, mythical.

Child 2: I think it might be a cross between real and mythical.

3. A Sign, Perhaps, that All Is Well

(In Which I Have Substituted) 'Poets' for 'Stones'

alteration of an artist statement by Ann Kuckelman Cobb;
found, Signs of Life Gallery, Lawrence

Before the children of Europe took these hills, the people
who walked here believed poets to be alive
because they carried heat, changed their forms,
and moved if you watched them long enough.
      – William Least Heat Moon

We think of poets as being solid, more or less
impervious to external forces, essentially "doing nothing."
But there is another way to think of poets:
as airy, aware, conscious – as purses
for time. Poets carry
information, patterns
from our ancient past, a secret code
that speaks of the way the world was,
and is.

Mourn the Cicadas

found graffiti, desk W15, 4½ Stacks, Watson Library, Kansas University

I have attained the Bird's Eye

And at the desk of the Duke begins a poet's journey

Earth below us, drifting, falling

I want to know about Organized Religion

I am not doing well

In the jungle / you must wait, / until the dice / read 5 or 8

BC + JA 4-EVA

War is cruelty. There is / no use in trying to reform it. / The crueler it is, / the sooner it can be over. – Gen. William Tecumseh Sherman

As if you could kill time / without injuring eternity.

We broke the steam whistle!

We used to wait

I can't talk to the walls, they're yelling at me; I can't talk to my wife, she listens to the walls. – RB, F-451

I don't know any of you people who write on desks in libraries, but we must all be poets…except for those fools who pledge eternal love with the goddam initials followed by '4-eva' – the only things that are eternal = Time and Change

And the corrosive friends whose breath is so close / it whistles, are changed to tattered pretexts / as a sign, perhaps, that all's well with us. – John Ashbery

Mourn the cicadas

Divide et Impera

I finally understand

Awareness: it pisses you off

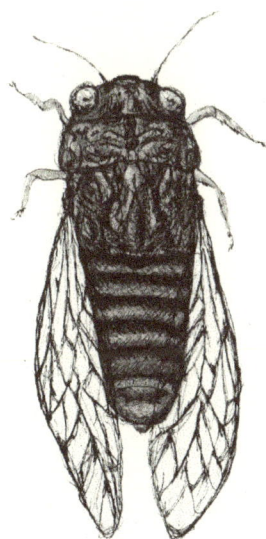

I Am Trying to Help You

overheard, receptionist on phone;
Douglas County Dental Clinic

I'm afraid
we don't do dentures.

No, we don't do dentures here, unfortunately.

Can I give you the number of a place you might try?

Well, like I said, we don't actually handle dentures.

No, we wouldn't be able to help you with that.

Can I go ahead and give you that number?
Affordable Dentures, in Topeka, would be
the place for dentures.

I'm sure they'd be able
to better answer those questions
over at Affordable Dentures. In Topeka.

I'm afraid I wouldn't be able to answer
any denture-related questions.

Let me give you the number.

The Transfer

overheard, woman on the #7 Bus, Lawrence

I'm gonna need a transfer, aren't I.
      I guess that's what always confuses me.
I don't know, I don't know
            why I can't get it
through my head. Too many
marbles lissing. Missing.
I guess. I don't know. I just…
Where are you gonna drop me off?
My schedule says you go to the Rec Center.
But that's 27th
      and Iowa. That's not where I live. Is it?
I'd need to get a transfer from there. Right?
            Where do I live? Behind
that old Shop-n-Save, or whatever it used to…at Iowa
and, what, 25th? Complex back behind there.
Didn't you drop me off there once? Or was it…
      That must've been the 8, then. I keep
missing that one. It's earlier than you.
            I'm always missing it for some reason.
I ran my errands today…picked up my meds…
      and then I guess I went in to the SandBar and got
talking with a guy I met there and he tried
            — well and anyway I guess I missed the 8
and had to wait 45, 55 minutes, I'd say,
and got this one, what is this, the 9?
The 7. I'm glad I caught you, at least.
            Where are you going again? I'm going
to have to get a transfer, aren't I. I guess that's what
gets me. I don't know. My
mind gets all…I just – am I going
to have to cross the street from Walgreens to get the next bus, or
cross the street *to* Walgreens. You tell me
what to do. That's why I get confused. It's the transfer.
I hate the transfer. You're absolutely *right* it's better
not to have the transfer – that's why
I like the Number 8: I can just sit there and wait till my stop.
I'm glad I got you, though, at least.

      But this time I'll have to transfer, won't I. You tell me
where. You'll tell me when to get out, right? You tell me.

The House Teetered On / The Edge of Absurdity

*found: thank-you card on ground; Java Break Café
and Cereal Bar, Lawrence*

Dear Mom Wolfe,

I just wanted to write
and thank you for three great
years at Phi Psi. You were
always there to provide
a presence of stability
and security when
the house teetered on
the edge of absurdity.
I know a lot of the guys
feel the same way. Thanks
for making Phi Psi feel
like home.

Sincerely,

Rustin Dodd
Class of '09

Postcard from Rose, 3, to Charlotte, 4, in Lawrence

Wamego, Kansas, 3-23-11

Dear Charlotte,

Today we went to the park in
Wamego. The seesaw thing was
more of a fast-ish, slow-ish thing.
Me and Daddy chased around the
windmill. There was an alligator
slide castle which was my favorite
thing. There was a pond and a
picnic house. We ate a sandwich and
cobbler. We went to the Oz Museum and
saw a haunted forest that had a Wicked
Witch in the corner of the ceiling.

       Your friend,
       Rose

Letter to Howard Payne

9 June, 2011

> *I have had to come so far away from it in order to understand it all!*
> – Lawrence Durrell

Dear Howard,

Please accept my apologies for the delayed response. My family and I have in fact survived the recent rash of tornados: the nearest hit was twenty miles away. However, things have still been a bit unsettled here, since my brother-in-law lost his job and car in Oklahoma and has taken up what seems to be a permanent residence on our sofa.

Nevertheless, I enjoyed the insight and wit of your Lawrence-themed letter – though I assure you this section of Kansas is not as flat as the part you must be remembering from your Beetle-bound cross-country spree to Sacramento. And yes, I suppose it's true that Judy Garland still drops in.

I'm not sure I knew you were in Oxford, or whether you know I was, too. Just a semester – 1997. Trimester, make that. Time enough, however, to become well acquainted with the pubs. So many pubs, and all flowing with divine bitter ale. It's where I learned to love lukewarm beer. I still have dreams of England's bars…though not, as far as I know, about its people. Perhaps this makes me shallow, or somewhat of an alcoholic. At least I'm not a hunchback! Although, that might make me more interesting. (Please tell more, if you're so inclined, about your time there and elsewhere in Europe, and of your odd comrades who both happened to be named Lawrence.)

Per your recommendations I have sought out and begun reading *Justine*, which I assumed was the natural spot to begin Durrell's quartet. It's no wonder you found it so eye-opening, given the rich description of place – as well as of the place of art in life.

Cheers, Howard. Say hello to your typewriter for me. I hope it's not too ornery these days.

Jeff

My Kin, My Country, My Casserole

Again with your picking around the broccoli, Jabez.
Blast it, don't you know there's kids storming in Normandy?
Casserole's meant to stay together, not to be sorted like tax
documents. There's no way around God's law,
Ezekiel. Jabez, I mean. And look at me, not at the TV.
Family, young man. It's what's good for you.
Green beans and carrots, too. And the Brussels sprout.
Heaven's bounty's found in relatives and vegetables.
I recall once during the war
jumping out of a chopper and landing at enemy HQ.
Kansas, it wasn't. It was some mountaintop
lair belonging to I-don't-know-who.
Must've been a very rocky region,
now that I think about it. But – anything for old Uncle Sam:
over land, over sea...*Over my dead body, pal.*
Pretty soon I had lead in my flank.
"Quick," I remember thinking, "how would FDR – or, LBJ –
respond in this situation?" Me, I
sat there bleeding like a jelly sandwich,
thinking how I'd miss Thanksgiving. Christmas. Eggnog.
Underpants knit by your dear grandmother – all that stuff
valued so much for its *traditional* value.

When far from home and close to death, your past's a wonderland.
Xanadu. Fond du Lac...

You better believe I escaped – and it wasn't by calling a cab.
Zeitgeist? Sure. Call it that. And finish your manna.

Without

Zoos that do not have at least one alpaca
yearn for completeness like a comb
x bristles short of a full row, or a Bic
without ink, or a deceased
ventriloquist whose puppet keeps speaking. These
utterances may bring grief
to those who are missing something,
someone. Sharks without teeth.
Rich folks and rock stars without some ennui.
Queens without kingdoms, or Brooklyn, at least. Jordan without a J.
Pitching great Nolan Ryan without a single K.
Or – what the hell – the city of Chicago without the El.
Nabokov – no: Humbert – without L-o-l-i-t-a. Wrigley without gum.
Mark Twain – the Mississippi, even – without Huck Finn.
Lennon without Yoko, and vice versa. Oh, no.
Kangaroos without the hop. Vesuvius without its top.
John Hancock, Esq. –
imagine the Declaration sans its most famous signer.
Hancock and his signatures
go hand in hand, it seems…but enough about that. Without
FDA approval, what would you
eat? Probably food you grew yourself, or TV
dinners imported illegally from low
countries. And speaking of completeness, here we are: let's have sex.
Because where would we be without *that*, baby?
Absent. Unborn. Unbegotten. Nowhere. Not Kansas, not Oz.

Zig Is My Name – Call This My Cantata

Yodeling's my passion. Don't laugh – some people comb
xanthan gum through their hair. Me, I merely warble in sync
with the waves of sound
vibrating and coursing through nature –
undulations that make life's stuff
teem and flourish and...*sing* –
songs of prosperity and fullness and growth –
robins and crows crooning tunes about cacti
quivering on the rooftops of the Taj –
palatial hymns that make one think
outlandish tales of merry canal-
nymphs, gleaming and a-swim,
melodious more for their form than their function.
Ladies – O! Ladies – of Amsterdam! Come back with me to
Kansas, where we'll sit on patios and sip
juice and speak not of the rise and fall of the NASDAQ –
its fluctuations are nothing compared to mine, my dear.
"Here," I'll say, "let me intone for you. Note how my notes
go up and down – how they seem to ricochet
from the highest peaks of Katmandu
east – or would it be west? – to the driest depths of the Negev –
down-down-up, down-down-*up*, high-high-*low* –
careening through the canyons like lox
bagels through weak intestines; like rotten turkey –"
and then they'll stop me and say, "Enough talk. Just sing, Z."

4. You Are Here

It Never Happens

It happens
every year at the end
of the season: the softball team
gathers in the parking lot
for beers and Mike
has too many or just enough
to start realizing he doesn't want it
to be over and it's over
already and the season was
way too short
and they should have
a Damn October League but by God he's going to have
the team over to his place, a team gathering*
in the offseason, so help him, who's in

and we all tell him of course
we're in, hell yes
we're in, we say

-

update:

2012:
* a team golf-outing

2013:
*a team fishing expedition, to Canada

Ours Was the Best-Dressed Scarecrow

We still have no idea where he got the Gucci suits.

Steadfast – and stately: that was our Henry.

He wore a dapper hat, tipped down to hide his eyes.

He always was discreet when it came to female callers.

At times we'd hear him whistling in the wind.

We asked him politely not to smoke those cigarettes.

Last night our Henry ascended in flames.

We shudder when we think

of what could happen next.

There were never crows here in the first place.

But who are we to say he hadn't kept it that way?

My Topeka Writers Group Leader Passed Out

My Topeka writers group leader passed out
a prompt to write "an epistle
to someone who inspires"
but I couldn't really think
of anyone specific
– though I did keep thinking
about my Topeka writers group
and how much I like it
(I mean *them*) and how
everyone's so nice and
welcoming and honest and people
even bring food and drinks to share, and paperclips,
and after I put that line break up there
between *passed out* and *a prompt*
I couldn't help but think
of my high school physics teacher, Mr. Zuidema,
who famously looked like Gargamel
but acted like the opposite of Gargamel –
funny and subtle and terribly
*un*sinister, that is –
and who also would famously pause and look around
after saying "I think I'm going to pass out"
and before saying "your quizzes now"
to see if anyone appeared concerned

William C. Quantrill

(Lawrence: August 21, 1863)

descends
with his crew
and his Q and his
You better get the hell out of my way
and even if you don't it's all the same I will roll
over your people and your buildings because sacks
are why I walk this earth and I won't think
twice before putting thirteen holes in the back
of your father's jacket as he tries to climb a fence
or shooting your youngest brother with his hands up
in surrender against the clear August sky
or dragging your old men and your boys from their homes
to destroy them in front of their mothers and wives
because this is not a raid it's a massacre
and your too-blue town is going down

Torn/ado

collaboration with Charlotte Tigchelaar, age 5

Lookout tower saw
the wind dance
and told.

All ran,
hid.

All safe.

Wait –

One person killed.

All that was destroyed

rebuild

Bacon Raised

Helen's Hilltop

A roadside biker bar
in Tonganoxie, Kansas.
A Saturday night.
It was Elvis's birthday and also that
of a guy named Mike.
The party was mostly for Mike – about whom
I knew next to nothing, other than that
he's a friend of a friend of my friend Shawn, and he shares
a birthday with the King
and reportedly also has a fifteen-foot statue
of Elvis in his front yard.

So this party
was mostly about Mike turning thirty
but there was definitely an Elvis theme, what with
the Blue Hawaiian rum-drinks, the pill-topped cupcakes,
and the peanut-butter-banana-and-bacon
birthday cake, which tasted way better
than you're probably imagining. I'm not sure
if Elvis was as fond of bacon as he was
of pills and the PB&B combination,
but someone sure seemed to think so
and I'm glad they did, because after
two cupcakes, a Moon Pie, and a slice
of the PB&B&B cake, just as I was wondering
how bad my beer would taste,
who should walk up but a lady with a plate-
ful of bacon strips, which of course
would serve as the perfect palate cleanser
and allow for a far more fearless transition
back to the PBR.

So there she stood with her silver platter,
holding it out with both hands. Some of us, reluctant,
had to be coerced. Others eagerly partook.
I said something about it feeling like communion.
Then there was laughter and someone else
said *The body of Christ*, and then someone else
and someone else, and there we stood,
bacon raised in a sort of toast,
and blasphemed, maybe, or remembered.

For the Love of God, Sean Kuno:

...I've never worked this hard to be somebody's friend...
– Letter, found 11-10-09, Lawrence

She writes to you from Topeka. Pours
it out neatly in black ink. Lays it
all on some thin blue lines
       and now it's there in your hands.

She wants to still be your friend.
She has no idea what she did
        – yet begs forgiveness.

The silence is getting to her head.

It's your move, Sean Kuno. What are you going to do?
Just please don't toss it all out your window
near the corner of 31st and Iowa.

It'll sit for days in the rain.
The envelope will turn
from white to gray.
The ink will bleed.

February: Mass Street

People brace
themselves against
the wind
their crutches
and others

A pile of blankets
shudders as we pass

"Dust in the Wind" on Repeat (January 2011)

Kansas / Kerry Livgren, 1977

Pieces of time are measured, but Time lives between the stars.
      – Theodore Worozbyt

I move
to Kansas and within
a month
I buy
the CD

I'm such
a tourist

Same old song
takes on
new meaning

This tune
seems to be standing
the tests of time

I'm trying
to do more than pass

Song for 2013

I.
In Henry's Coffeeshop and almost everywhere else,
it's December 31, 2012.
A guy just walked up
and gave me two dinosaur stickers.
"They're from a 1985 *Highlights for Kids*," he said.

II.
New Year's Eve, 2012,
and on the brim of twenty thirteen
I want nothing more
than for you to be here
another year

Postcard, with Arrows

You Are Here
is the opposite
of Here You Are

Here you are, going
through the motions

Here you are, spinning
your wheels
sitting indoors
going on and on

until you decide to take off,
get up and out and go
and go until you are
There, There
being
where you want
to be, where you know
you're meant to dwell,
so much so
that you want to tell
the rest of the world
the news of your location,
your arrival.

ACKNOWLEDGMENTS

The author is grateful to the editors and readers of the following publications, in which these poems previously appeared:

"Report to William Stafford," *The Southeast Review*
"You Are Here," *seveneightfive*
"*from* Day Notes: Lawrence, Kansas," *Phoebe*
"All That's Happened since Kristen Spilled Beer on Our Carpet," *burntdistrict*
"Least Weasel (*Mustela nivalis*)," *Gertrude*
"Poem on Placard for Placard for Statue," *Sugar House Review*
"Reading at the Raven," *Blue Island Review*
"Today We Saw a Man," *Crab Creek Review*
"Fly Frontier," *Heavy Feather Review*
"The Thing about Dying," *Hawai`i Pacific Review*
"Dude, You Killed a Marsupial," *Hobart*
"George Brett's Labradoodle," *Hobart*
"There's This Thing," *Heavy Feather Review*
"Mourn the Cicadas" (as "A Sign, Perhaps, that All Is Well"), *The American Poetry Journal*
"The Transfer," *El Paper*
"The House Teetered On / The Edge of Absurdity," *Found Magazine*
"Letter to Howard Payne" (as "Howard: 9 June 2011"), *The Dirty Napkin*
"Without," *North American Review*
"Zig Is My Name – Call This My Cantata," *Grist*
"Ours Was the Best-Dressed Scarecrow," *Thrush Poetry Journal*
"William C. Quantrill," *I-70 Review*
"Bacon Raised," *Openings* (Trinity Christian College)
"For the Love of God, Sean Kuno," *Kansas City Voices*
"Postcard, with Arrows," *seveneightfive*

"Report to William Stafford" was reprinted in *A Ritual to Read Together: Poems in Conversation with William Stafford* (Woodley Press)

"Least Weasel" appeared in audio format on the *Lawrence Journal-World* web site

"Abandon" and "Stop" were published on the Cave Moon Press web log, edited by Doug Johnson

"Animals Were Looking at Me" was published in *Prairie Gold: An Anthology of the American Heartland* (Ice Cube Press)

Thank you to the following people, places, and things – for (what else) being there:

Matthew Porubsky, Shawn Tracy, Joe Snapper, Becca J.R. Lachman, Jennifer Schomburg Kanke, Kathryn Nuernberger, Jaswinder Bolina, Kristen Lillvis, Leah Sewell, Bao Phi, Mark Halliday, Wyatt Townley, Denise Low, Eric McHenry, Jim Daniels, Dennis Etzel Jr., Mary Stone, Jeff Cunningham, Cathy Runyon, Mike Wyngarden, Sheila McGrath, Jill Read, Mark Hennessy, Brian Daldorph, Phil Wedge, Mary Klayder, Kevin Rabas, Megan Kaminski, Jessica Conoley, Maryfrances Wagner, Nedra Rogers, Ryan Bradley, Alice Friman, Michael Vander Weele, and Virginia LaGrand

The Raven Bookstore, The Lawrence Arts Center, J&S Coffee, The Java Break, Signs of Life Books & Art, Donkey Coffee and Espresso, and The Writers Place

The Ohio Arts Council, The Topeka Writers Group, Washburn University and Woodley Press, Advance Newspapers, The Athens News, The Lawrence Journal-World, and the English departments at Trinity Christian College, Ohio University, and The University of Kansas

I would also like to thank my parents, Don and Jan Tigchelaar, and my brothers, Steve Tigchelaar and Mark Tigchelaar

as well as Charlotte Pemberton for her artistic vision and initiative

Jeremy Shellhorn for stepping in and turning it all out

and again, of course, especially:

Jana

About the author

Jeff Tigchelaar is a former newspaper reporter, editor, and stay-at-home dad. His poems have been published in Kansas, Canada, Germany, and Wales, as well as on bar coasters. He blogs for *XYZ Topeka* and currently works as a paraeducator at Southwest Middle School in Lawrence.

About the illustrator

Charlotte L. Pemberton is an illustrator, printmaker, and Kansas native. She currently resides in Lawrence, Kansas, with her family.

www.ingramcontent.com/pod-product-compliance
Lightning Source LLC
Chambersburg PA
CBHW051848040426
42447CB00006B/746